WORLD HAPPINESS INDEX

WORLD HAPPINESS INDEX

Poems

KATHLEEN AGUERO

Cover image: "The Joy of Youth," photo © Glen McClure. www.GlenMcClure. com.

Published by Tiger Bark Press,
202 Mildorf Ave., Rochester, NY 14609.

Edited and published by Steven Huff.
Typeset and designed by Philip Memmer.

ISBN-13: 979-8-9853587-0-4

In memory of HJ Aguero

For Richard, for my children Robert and Veronica,
and for my grandchildren, Damion, Emory, Savannah, and Nicholas

Contents

III

I

THE WORLD HAPPINESS INDEX, 2019

How happy I am to live
in the nineteenth happiest country in the world.
Tulips rose this month through the arsenic soil,
and the air I breathe is dark with money. In country nineteen
we can say what we want. A professor in California
is allowed to say we elected a racist president,
and those who disagree can leave phone messages
threatening his nine-year-old daughter because we live
free or die. Our children leave their houses each morning happy,
not knowing what adventures the day holds. Might they be shot
on the sidewalk by an officer who mistakes
their cell phone for a gun or by a stray
bullet in the playground? Or will they get
to school where they can hide in the closet
from an "active shooter"? If they arrive home safely,
there's always tomorrow, and maybe tomorrow
their teachers will have guns. They are happy
to be living in this just-happy-enough country
where no one dares get sick for fear
of bankruptcy. If you try in happy country nineteen,
you too can be as rich as the sea, and if not,
there are lots of street corners to live on
and happy things to swallow or snort,
and the fetid air from the subway grate
will keep you warm at night if you knock someone
else off it playing King of the Mountain.
We have problems, of course, that we're trying to solve,
but we're from the country of hard work and initiative,
of take what you want and say it was yours
all along. Numbers one, two, and three
with their orderly lives, their health care,
and housing and good schools for free,

grow soft and mushy. Not us.
We're the ice inside a snowball,
the rubber hose that leaves no mark.
We dance on the head of uncertainty,
cruelty's pin. Every morning our sun rises,
red, white, and blue.

FEAR STREET

I lived on Main Street in a quiet city,
where citizens spoke kindly
of those they didn't have to live with,
but underneath every complacent surface
is a set of fangs, sharp and growing sharper.
Hungry, irritable, insatiable.
How suddenly it seemed to draw back
its lips. I didn't see it coming.
They said that's because you didn't
have to. It wasn't gnawing on you.
How indignant I was on their behalf.
How I loved my indignation.
They rolled their eyes at my innocence
which was expensive and costing
their lives. But I'd never hurt you,
I said. We all live on Fear Street,
they replied, but you couldn't read
the sign. We're all being swallowed.
Go ahead, if you don't believe us,
walk into its maw.

CROAGH PATRICK

after a photograph by Glen McClure

Fog slips down the holy mountain, a soft shawl
halting just above tree line while from the sky and open water
dark clouds like claws reach
toward the quiet house, still pasture.
The corrugated water of the bay, waves barely raising their knuckles,
will soon swell to pummel the shore. On Reek Sunday,
pilgrims climb Croagh Patrick to honor the saint
who fasted forty days on its summit. Some trudge barefoot
to atone for their sins. Cleansed but bloodied,
they return, carried on pallets.

No pilgrims this day. The gap in the clouds filling
with storm about to break through the camera's frame.

STREET SONNET

A woman, middle finger lifted high,
screams curses at the sky. Her fraying clothes
mismatched, shoes loose, blouse torn awry:
a rank sibyl, shouting. Does she suppose
the sun's to blame for beggars in the streets
or for the kids who mock her from their car
matching the obscenities with which she greets
them? She must suspect what cowards we are,
our faces blank as if we haven't heard
their *stupid bitch,* her frenzied *fuck you too,*
which make us walk more quickly. It's absurd
the way we turn our heads, avoid her view.
Too timid to speak up or meet her gaze,
we smooth our hair. Her anger sears the day.

LIBERTY HOTEL, BOSTON

*We didn't want to lose our jailness," says Dillon, "but we wanted
to do it [renovate jail into a hotel] in a way that didn't come across
as dark.*
                                    —From *Lockdown Luxury,* Ann Coppola

Cell to cell in saffron robes, Buddhist monks
bless the Liberty Hotel. Their chants cover
the echoes of inmates shouting at Frankie entering
the room where he'll spend five weeks
in solitary, naked in the six by eight cell,
four walls slimy with mold. Frayed rope
dangles from the ceiling of the luxury suite.
Incense circles the guards.

Look: Frankie, just finished his bid,
passes the bellhops carrying bags,
the concierge calling cabs, as he
approaches the day officer's barred window,
collects his clothes, his watch, then exits
the prison doors. He blinks through the exhaust
of the traffic circle at Buzzy's Roast Beef across the way
and, eyeing the keys, chats with a valet parking cars.

Hang a "Solitary" sign on the doorknob,
sleep safe beneath blankets that mimic
the ones Nicola Sacco clutched to his chin.
Under the ocular windows, relax on darkened catwalks
glamorous with loveseats, tables for two.
Nearby, Malcolm, in his cellblock, studies
W.E.B. Dubois, *The Souls of Black Folk.*
We'll eat dinner at the Clink,
*where vestiges of original cells
create cozy nooks,* and Bartolomeo Vanzetti,
silently rehearsing his speech to the court,

orders filet mignon from a waiter in a uniform
stenciled with Malcolm's old number, 22843.
But, first, cocktails in the former drunk tank,
re-named Alibi, which we now think we have.
We, too, can experience *jailness* at the Liberty Hotel,
though we wouldn't recognize any of them—
not Sacco, Vanzetti, Malcolm X, not Frankie
biting into his first roast beef in years.

SPELLING LESSON

The first word is "fear." The second, "fare," as in "How do you fare today, class?" And the third word is "pharaoh"—a trick! Why are they out of alphabetical order? That's what happens when you're afraid. Things get jumbled. Have you already forgotten the first word? Are you frightened yet? If I'm moving too fast for you, we'll go back to an earlier book. The next word is "anxiety." As in—anxiety colors everything. Can you spell it? Taste it? Feel it clog your throat and clamp your stomach? The bright sun is menacing, the sales clerk is about to laugh at you, back home you've left the iron on, the front door unlocked, and your only child is running across the street without looking. He's in the blind spot of the oil truck backing out of the driveway. Only one thing can happen next. You've cautioned him about that spot a thousand times; you let him go alone against your better judgment. Quick—tell me where you really are! Not quick enough. I'll call on someone else. Very good, the classroom. Now I want you to relax, give in to your anxieties, and if that paradox makes you nervous the next word is "panic." Spell the past tense of the verb "to panic." Your spelling's fine, but your understanding somewhat limited, for once you've passed anxiety and fear there's no past tense to panic. Just when you're relaxing—go ahead, spell "relaxing" just for fun, but faster, faster, it doesn't last for long—just when you are "r-e-l-a-x-i-n-g" up pops panic. Feel it come and go like radio reception in the mountains.

OCTOBER IN SALEM

On the first of the month, banks of porta-potties appear on every main street. Traffic grows thicker each day. Cars block the crosswalks; pedestrians step heedlessly into the road. A Batmobile drives down New Derby St. Not a parking meter to be found, and nearly every side street plastered with orange stickers: *Resident Parking Only.* Schools and enterprising homeowners rent out their spots. A costumed couple exits a van on our street. They've driven all the way from Toronto and can't find anywhere to leave their car. I assure them no one will ticket here. Just up the road, tourists exit buses whose license plates read "New Jersey" and "Montreal." Two witches from Florida have their photo taken with me in my haphazard costume—sequined mask, fancy hat with veil. A fanged werewolf tells me he's traveled here from Finland, but no one is as frightening as the local dressed in black who pushes a broken-down buggy holding a bloodied baby doll into the diner. Other women wear elaborate witch hats in velvet or satin, colorful flowers and fake fruit on the band, spiders embroidered on the black veils covering their faces or small hats attached to plastic head bands, jaunty as the fascinators British princesses wear—purely ornamental, covering nothing, and nothing like hats worn by those drowned or burned as actual witches. The memorial behind the museum bears their names: *Bridget Bishop, Hanged June 10, 1692; John Proctor, Hanged August 19, 1692.* An inscription reads: *On my dying day, I am no witch.* Next to the memorial is Old Burying Point, where lies John Hathorne, the hanging judge, but the cemetery is closed to prevent it from being trampled by tourists. Tragedy and celebration mingle the way smoke from piles of burning leaves mixes in the air, sharing a certain frenzy. The giddy throngs waver between make believe and why not believe. Witch is the magic preface here: witch candles, witch soap, witch herbs, and coat hooks. Even police cars bear the logo of a witch on a broomstick. My friend from Norway snaps a photo. *People must love you,* she tells the officer. *Yeah, right,* he says and rolls his eyes. On the pedestrian mall, Frankenstein checks his cell phone. When he takes a coffee break, he posts a large sign that reads *Do not sit or climb on Frankenstein's chair.* No one is dressed as Proctor or Bishop.

THEM

They should have left
town, gone
quietly, followed directions,
paid attention, studied
our map, re-calculated.

They should have known
their days were numbered.
Our time had come.
They could have stayed
on their own side
and said nothing,
been agreeable, like us.
(They could never
be like us.) They should have
worked harder, joined the ranks,
read the fine print, signed
the dotted line, changed
their accents, paid in cash.

They smelled like garlic,
wore strange clothes,
reneged on agreements
then said we didn't keep
our word. They complained too much.
What else were we to do?

HAPPY SKIES SPA: REFLEXOLOGY

A neon halo shines above a flashing foot
but when I go inside to buy
a gift certificate for my daughter,
a young woman, sleek fall of dark hair,
shakes her head, adamant in struggling
English: *No reflexology. Bodywork.*
Only bodywork. Back at home—no websites.
Just online reviews on rubmaps.com: *Beautiful masseuse.*
Try the table shower. It's the balls. To read more pay and join.

I read about a family that traded their daughter
for enough money to stop death threats from loan sharks.
Does this really happen:
fields poisoned; son
dead; daughter
on a plane to us?

She could be inside that storefront
where the shades are always drawn
and the sign reads *Massage* or *Bodywork*.
No doubt the ones who took her discovered
all her useful attributes: her hands, her mouth, her pretty
unlined face.

The weekend detective gives me the number
of the day detective. The day detective takes a message
for the night detective. No one calls back.
On the FBI hotline a woman answers: *rubmaps... usually a tip-off.*
Was there an ATM? Were the windows shuttered?
Here's the reference number. May we contact you?

A month later, the night detective leaves a message.
Assures me, *It's under control.* And me—
white lady in a down coat and boots, appalled,
calling the police, the FBI, then warming up a plate
of fragrant stew, what am I prepared
to understand? That young woman
gets arrested. Another takes her place.

THIRTEEN WAYS OF LOOKING AT A GHAZAL

While birdsong spans the air like a ghazal,
day flutters open, a fan, a ghazal.

Spare change, homeless, the veteran
pleads. I hand him a ghazal.

Though long ago I gave up prayer,
I cannot quit the Stations of the Ghazal.

When the fleeing children moan
I bandage them with ghazals.

May the mourning mother's tears
expand this ghazal.

At the wedding, guests exhaust themselves
dancing the electric ghazal.

While her lover plays his passion out,
her mind drifts, branching like a ghazal.

Before the ballgame the poets rise
to sing the Star Spangled Ghazal.

It may look like a U-Haul the salesman claims
but it handles like a ghazal.

Among twenty striving poems, the only dazzling syllables
play the fandango of the ghazal.

Even William Carlos Williams admits
you can get the news from ghazals.

Of all the treasures we have filched
the grandest is the ghazal.

What! Mizra Ghalib protests,
Kathleen, stop mangling this ghazal.

TO THE CHILDREN AT THE BORDER

*...an unprecedented 69,550 migrant children held in U.S.
government custody over the past year*
—AP news, Nov. 12, 2019

You waver, pale shades at the edge
of a crowd of costumed children calling
Trick or Treat. Pots of bright asters
sit on front steps. Plastic skeletons
hang from trees. As the season changes
in a blaze of excitement, mock terror,
I imagine you, children caged
at the border of my country.

When my grandson kicks his soccer ball
down the wide cul-de-sac, and it rolls on the lawn
of a neighbor who smiles indulgently, I picture
your neighbors, guards, patrolling with guns.
When the toddler sneaks macaroni
from his brother's plate and, grinning, pops it
into his own mouth, I imagine your deep hunger,
your delicate bones straining
against your skin. When the baby wails
for mama who rushes over and lifting her baby
kisses her cheek, I hear your mothers'
cry, arms exhausted from their emptiness,
and wonder if your eyes are too dry for tears.

With the children of my blood, I hollow
a pumpkin, and together we pull the wet seeds
and stringy membranes out with our hands,
now covered with its gore. We place a candle
inside it so the grimace we carved
flickers with menace. I try to bring you into focus

as your image trembles like the light inside that pumpkin.
Does it matter I know you are there? And tomorrow—
Dia de Todos los Santos, Dia de los Angelitos.

MAINTAIN CONTROL OF YOUR LUGGAGE

at all times. Do not let it
roll through the airport
unattended. Likewise when you get home,
curb your dog, your children.
Don't let them near your neighbors' yards.
While you're at it, why not control
your neighbors as well? Be sure
they observe the correct times
for putting out trash and taking it in,
keep their lawns mowed, their houses painted
the prescribed colors. Report transgressions
to the Neighborhood Association. Be suspicious
of anyone who rings your doorbell
pretending to be lost. Even a child
can cause harm. If someone makes you nervous,
well, you're allowed to protect yourself
in this country. If they're on your property,
better safe than sorry. We have laws.
Make sure those laws are on your side of the street.
The one you control. The street's not wide enough
for everyone. Rezone, if you must.
That's how it works and be careful
who you rent to. If you can't
understand their accents, they may cheat
you, and the strange smell of their food
will linger in your house. Make sure
their suitcases are packed in case
you need them to leave.
Face it: we can't control everything.
That's why we have rules in this country.

THE RIDER/THE HORSE

Fear saddled me, trained me,
stabled me, named me,
braided my hair.
Carrot and stick,
taught me to dance,
taught me to rear,
shod me and hobbled me,
bred me and pastured me,
cantered me, galloped me,
spurred me and drove me
out of the meadow
into the thicket,
out of the thicket
into the woods.
Fear held the bridle,
tightened the bit.
Fear was the master
brutal and quick,

but was I the horse?
Was I the rider?

AT SIXTEEN MONTHS: BROWN AND GOLD

My grandson plucks a marigold
poking through a neighbor's white fence,
crushes it between his fingers
while I try to remember
if it's poisonous. Three days later
he's alive, so I cross the marigold
off my list of potentially lethal flora
toddlers might put in their mouths.
So far, he has not harmed himself
by falling while carrying a stick
and poking out his eye, something
my mother assured me would happen
if I ever ran with a stick in my hand.
Though he tugs hard at the baby gate,
he has not pulled it down. Though he has banged
on the window, he has not shattered it,
cut himself, or fallen to the pavement
two stories below. His skin has not
turned from brown to blue
during a tantrum, and he has grabbed
the dog's whiskers without being bitten.
He bulldozes his way. He prods
and he pushes. He tries to put the whole
of the dangerous world in his mouth
while I follow ready to snatch
the worst away. When tired,
he wobbles, he falls, he cries,
but the next day he's walking again.
Golden marigold petals stain his brown hand
as he carries his stick. So far
no one thinks it's a gun.

NEGATIVE SPACE: COVID 19

I reach toward my friend
when she confides her bad news,
then pull my hand back
subtracting touch.
The quotient is empathy
divided by safety. Add six feet
to any operation. A hemisphere
of empty arms the symbol of a hug,
arms around the self, the binomial
of caring. I forget all the time
the equation of breath multiplied
by the velocity of wind lessened
by time spent together. If my sigh
leaves my mouth a moment
after she's spoken and hers exits
two seconds later will they cross
in the danger zone, and which of us
is more worried? I step away.
The circumference of friendship
distorted. Touch always more
than the sum of its parts.

II

SELF-PORTRAIT

I live in a land of trash
and extravaganza. I know

the party's over by used condoms
and empty nip bottles rolling in the street.

If today held one thing worth remembering
I forgot to look for it. I tell myself

don't wear out like a sequined dress
split at the seams, dropping glitter.

Luckily no one notices
so I don't get discarded.

Disapproval, a heavy coat
I'm afraid to shrug off.

Stop. The event I dread will be here
soon enough. Why wear myself

thin as a sheet?

MUTE SELF-PORTRAIT

If only a hibiscus bloomed from my mouth
If flame
If my words persuaded
like ice in a heat wave
my voice poured like a waterfall
down a silver slope
and a hurricane roared from my throat

But not this stuck stone,
this mouth filled with grit
When I speak sand floats
through the air and the room
is covered with dust

SELF-PORTRAIT AS SUN WASHED

A watery, whisper-soft shade, this lovely pale peach is
reminiscent of fine vintage lace and heirloom embroidery.
　　　　　—Benjamin Moore online paint catalog.

So pale maybe "about to faint"
would be a better name
or "pink-shirt-washed-too-many times."
Unlike the sun, this color lacks conviction.
Name it "boring-day-in-a-long-marriage,"
"daily chores." Name it "me-at-a-liminal
-time in my life" or "neither-here-nor-there."
Name it "too-timid-to-be-seen," "nearly invisible,"
"woman past the middle of her life".

SELF-PORTRAIT AS VILLANELLE

It's too much, too little, too big, too small—
The voice in your head a persistent drum—
Not enough, too many, too short, too tall.

Quit your whining the same voice growls.
Push the mantra you chant to a distant hum.
It's too much, too little, too big, too small.

Give it too much gas and make it stall.
Hold its head under water to drown its thrum:
Not enough, too many, too short, too tall.

Your problem is that you want it all.
But see for yourself, when you think you've won,
It's too much, too little, too big, too small.

If you picture yourself, you want to crawl
Into a tunnel where you try to outrun
Not enough, too many, too short, too tall.

Could you muffle that voice with a widow's shawl?
Could you stare it down till it's nearly dumb?
No, it's too much, too little, too big, too small.
Not enough, too many, too short, too tall.

SELF-PORTRAIT AS GERANIUM

Here's all I've got:
one showy cluster of red blossoms,
fancy hat on a scrawny neck
rising above bare stems and gently ruffled leaves
with their dark inner border, peach fuzz. Leggy, untrimmed,
I'm Americana Red in a green plastic pot.
A scatter of brown blooms
dusts the soil beneath me.

I know how I must look
straining toward the window
close enough to tap it,
better yet, break through.
Look at me. Let me out.
Look at me. Let me out.
Petals weighing nothing.

SELF-PORTRAIT AS THE TWO OF SWORDS

Again, for my birthday, you lay out the cards.
By now you know all the things
I want to change but don't. Each year
I get the two of swords, blindfolded woman,
her back to the sea, crescent moon in the sky,
and each year you point out she could uncross her arms,
drop those swords, untie her blindfold, leave.

I don't want to be her,
hoodwinked figure who can't tell
she's free, but, if change were easy,
wouldn't she turn to look
at the moon and the sea?
She's perfectly balanced. What she can't see
can't hurt her. Her hands, always full,
will never be the devil's playthings.
But don't her arms ache lifting those swords?
What muscles she must have from raising them so long.

You've moved to the next card
while I nod as if I believe this time,
with your urging, I'll reach behind my head,
untie that knot, become the woman of "Strength"
hand on the lion's mouth without fear,
or "The Star," graceful maiden,
effortlessly pouring water from two pitchers,
one foot in the pool, one knee on the earth.

SELF-PORTRAIT AS FEATHER DUSTER

You brought me home compact,
then loosed my thick feathers
over your tabletops, windowsills,
figurines, clocks. I harvest
dead skin, shed hair, lint you nervously
pick from your clothes. Now everything's
fresh as your youth.

                Back in the closet,
no one notices me, strange bird,
no beak, no claws. At night
I rise light as dandelion silk.
I twirl and send your dirt flying.
Next morning a flock of gray motes
swirls in the sun's rays that stream
through your window revealing
my glory. *Ashes to ashes,*
I sing. *Dust to dust.*

PORTRAIT IN SEARCH OF ITSELF

A vacant lot. A blank-faced rubber doll
that only speaks when baby pulls the cord.
A mirror shines its light when people look
reflecting what it is they want to see.
A hall of mirrors multiplies their dance,
but what is it when no one is around?
Great Zoltan shut inside a square glass box
will turn his head—here, put a token in,
pick up his phone. He'll let you know just what
your future holds then wait mechanical,
immobile and mute. A kettle's still
until you light the flame to make the water
whistle for your tea. Then it subsides.
A half-filled pot. A saucer left behind.

SELF-PORTRAIT AS ANGRY DOG

Steal the roast
Shit on the carpet
Roll in something dead
Lick my balls
Mangy fur scabby
Fleas
Hot slobber
Carrion breath
Lips pulled back
Yellowed teeth
Growl snarl
Foam
Pull at the leash
Break the chain
Leap for the throat
All of it

SELF-PORTRAIT AS SEAGULL

Forget the jittery plover
nesting in the sand, just asking
for its eggs to be crushed
by your careless foot, nervously
darting away and deserting its young
if you come near. Picture me
on an inflatable lounger
knocking ash from my cigar,
gin and tonic handy.
Trash-talking marauder
screeching with my gang in intertidal pools,
I play chicken as you walk the shore,
snatch your lunch from its paper bag.
Look for me in the parking lot
behind the market where I street fight
over clams, then strut,
a piece of shell hanging from my beak.

SELF-PORTRAIT AS EMPTY BOAT

Moored prayer.
Cup to be filled
on the palm of the water.

Silent promise.
Open mouth. Breath exhaled.
A dream before

it begins. Crest and plunge—
the wave's outburst

THE EMPTY BOAT SPEAKS

Water licking my ankles
Salt's slow finger down my back

Sanded by the wave's rough tongue
Then a long ride down a slow swell
a short slide down a whale's fin
my spine a keel, a skate's egg case—
that's what I wanted when I entered the water

The current pulled but I rose
seasoned, warped,
hold-slosh, smell of low tide

SELF-PORTRAIT AS RIVER

Body elongated
sunlight stippled
Metal smell
Mud stir
The swollen
The fertile
The dried-up bed

Stroked smooth
or wind whipped
over rocks churning
pushing sticks gathering
force flooding
then pooled placid
whatever weather makes me

SELF-PORTRAIT AS SUNRISE

Here I am:
can-can girl high-kicking
night out of the sky. Coral skirts,
hot pink feather boa, arms draped
across that electric navy horizon.
Dazzle dance, quick flirt, fade, and gather
my skirts into that spiked circle
children paint in the corner
of their pictures. That thing
you think you know.

III

DIFFICULT CHILD

In the kitchen, my neighbor's young daughter climbed on a chair,
pulled a dull knife from the counter, and threatened
to kill herself. Her parents sat in the den,
and when I rose said, *The doctor told us,*
ignore her until she calms down.
She was the difficult child. I went in.
She put down the knife.

I understand her, what she was doing and why
her parents didn't rise from their chairs;
I understand the pull of the empty threat and the threat
of the empty threat. I was the difficult child
who hid outside in the dark, so my parents
couldn't find me. *We were about to call the police,*
my father said. The little girl grew to trust
the dream catcher she hung over her bed
would capture nightmares,
let good dreams slip through.

I trust the dream:
the one in which my sister finds
in the bedtable drawer my mother's
gold necklace that I'd misplaced,
and there it is when I wake. The dream
where I lean across the table
toward a woman in shadow and say,
Grandma, neither of us has that much time;
the one where my friend walks beside me
on the bike path then says, *Stay here,*
and heads back to her death.
And the one in which my neighbors

enter the kitchen where their daughter
is doing the dance of the knives,
and they admire her skill, her magical feet,
the quick flash of steel. Their arms
around her, all of us dance.

SHE

Outside, the hurricane. Inside she,
pacing, cursing her broken left wrist,
all she can't do with just one hand. Outside,
the large limb of a maple, snapped,
one end caught on a power line, the other
balanced on her car which can't be moved
lest the limb fall and the power line break. Inside,
she wants to escape, walk in the angry weather
but when she opens the door, firefighters shout,
Live wire. Back inside.
Inside with the man who shouts at the firefighters,
Don't just stand there. Do something.
When the rain quiets, she opens the window,
hears her neighbors calling to one another
from their front porches. She wants to join,
but as she heads out to the street, they point
to the line dangling in front of her house:
Go back in. Go back in. The man inside
has stopped sulking. He's on the phone talking
then quietly sketching in his small book. She
puts dishes away with one hand, wanting to chip them,
bang lids against pans, be blown away
by the wind before it dies down.

YOU

Did it begin with the sky holding back its rain like a fist
stopping just short of your face, the slight rush
of air on your jaw? You'd rather a thunderhead's anvil
stalking as you back into a room
with a lock, because that actual fist
clenched round a storm could let loose,
break down the door. Now you're stuck
in the bathroom trying to retrace the map
that got you here. You lean on the wall,
slide to the floor as the shouting grows stronger,
loud bang on the door. If you climbed out the window
where would you go? How could you run
carrying that heavy sky on your shoulders?

HE

finds a window, fogs it with breath, traces his initials. Briefly he mono-grams the sky as if he owned it. He's a smudge already vanishing against glass. The tattoo on his arm crepes and sags. The fist he ruled with crowned by arthritic knuckles. If he had it to do over, he would. At fif-teen, he grabbed a shard of the bottle his father had thrown and gripped it till his palm bled, relishing the salt of pain. After that, the circling truce of two street cats, evenly matched. He'd used what he'd been giv-en—strong legs and arms—to muscle his way through the crowd. If he'd smashed everything he suspected he loved—some purity in that. Why should he care his initials are gone from the glass? He'd never chased the sky with its bland blessings but searched torn paper wrappers, used condoms, broken bricks for his name.

AFTER A DREAM OF BETRAYAL

anger and grief flash through your body
like a neon sign. Your husband lies near
with his contented warmth, his trusting
breath, but your body stiffens and turns away.
Caught in the dream's rip tide, you have
to resist struggle, swim parallel
until the current slackens,
lets you roll back to the sleeper beside you
dreaming the mutual shore.

PRAISE FOR THE ILL

(Reiki at Brigham and Women's Hospital)

Praise to the patient,
who says of the winter's cold,
I wouldn't choose to be here
but at least I'm in a warm, dry bed,
to the woman in elegant pajamas
waiting for a transplant who asks me how I am,
to the young one with the beautiful eyes
and thinning hair who smiles when she tells me
she'll be here for six months and wonders if her mother
sent me, to her brother sitting by her bed
in a mask, checking his email, to all those
who allow me to touch them and to the patient
swollen from burns, skin crackling
like a thanksgiving turkey's who trusts me
not to touch her, to the hallucinating girl who sees bugs
crawling toward her and lets me brush them away.
To the ones who fidget, the ones who fall asleep,
to those who say no and those who say yes,
to the woman who told me, *your hands are so warm.*
At first I thought it must be the work of the devil.
To the body's frailty and to its strength,
to the great generosity of the ill, to the calm
they bring me, to their tubes and their wires,
their beeping machines, Purell, gloves, masks,
and gowns, a list of precautions on each of their doors,
an icon of someone falling, high risk.
To women whose flanks poke out
from their hospital gowns, so lost in their beds
I hardly can find them, to men
so tall their feet push at the foot rail,

and to the man whose mechanical heart
shakes the bed. As the sky darkens,
they struggle to sleep, each breath
dedicated to a single purpose.

RADIOLOGY WAITING ROOM

The young volunteer enters uncertainly, carrying a cardboard box of craft supplies. She's planned projects to lift our spirits while we wait yet again for our machine to get fixed. I lean close to the others who meet here each day. We want to keep advising the newcomers, hear from those who started before us about the best ointment for the sores that come next. We want to complain about traffic and broken machines, but she sits down, her face tender as the new moon, and soon Alice, grandmother of five, takes pity and starts folding an origami crane.

I preferred the volunteer who came with a puppy, soft fur in a crate, or even the one with the snake in a box. We all loved the toddler who banged on the glass tank startling the tropical fish and played peek-a-boo with us across an aisle of chairs while his father adjusted the scarf slipping from his wife's bald head.

Just as today's volunteer approaches my chair with her paper squares the technician calls. He winks and mouths *saved you*. As I lay myself like a chop on the table, pull the johnnie off my right arm baring my breast, we laugh. We know if she'd reached me, I'd be folding a crane.

MY BARGAIN

I discover my right breast
on the dented can shelf,
no longer the full 16 ounces,
a little flat on one side,
a little scratched near the nipple.
I take it down, blow off the dust,
examine it from every angle,
weigh it in one hand, hold it up to my left side—
not a match, but close enough—then think of all the junk
in my closet, pilled sweaters, single socks,
unworn thrift store finds. About to turn away,
I hear my mother's voice, *What a deal!*
I slip it under my coat,
leave without paying.

DOG DAYS

That the vehicles we are given
in which to survive would be these
bothersome bodies, harder to maintain
than a house, impossible to trade in
like a car. Nor do they appreciate
in value, no matter how our minds
may soar (but the mind, too, loses
a word here, a detail there). These bodies
fall down around us, take more and more
time to keep up. We doze in the sun
like old dogs remembering the sleek hounds
we once were. Now and then one leg quivers
as we catch a scent of the past.

COASTAL FOG

At Tofino, fog, an invisible cloak.
I'm lost, but not lost. If I turn around
I'll be back where I started. Though I can't see
where I started. In a plane how I've wanted
to put my hand out the window, touch a cloud.
Now a fog coat, a dream on my skin. Fog
an invading army of silence. Self-absorbed,
it absorbs self-absorbed me. Its song so quiet
only moths can hear it. We invent mournful horns
to speak in its place. Coastal fog,
roll me up in your arms,
before sun burns us through.

SPYING

is what I love, not as a voyeur, not in the sense that I'm getting away with something, seeing what I shouldn't. But the small window frame, the yellow light, the comfort of people going about their ordinary lives—a girl reading on the sofa, a man setting groceries on the table... Once I saw a woman peeling carrots into the kitchen sink, her long earrings swaying forward as she leaned. She looked as if she were humming to herself, as if her soul were lounging far away while her hands worked rhythmically and thin, dirty carrot skins dropped into the sink.

This has nothing to do with loneliness, either. Suppose I had been sitting at her kitchen table, her guest, watching her prepare a meal, drinking a beer with her, laughing, cherished. That dreaminess would not be there; the essence of herself would be put to one side as we focused on each other and on ourselves focusing on each other. But looking through the window I am effaced, a distraction neither to myself nor to this woman who can drift and have her drifting honored.

BETTER SELF

There was a little girl,
    Who had a little curl,
Right in the middle of her forehead.
When she was good,
    She was very good indeed,
But when she was bad,
She was horrid
             —Henry Wadsworth Longfellow

When I'm bored by some slow dinner story,
about to say, *Get to the point,*
my better self interrupts, *Please pass the peas,*
then tugs the choke collar. My better self
makes excuses for me: *I don't know what's got into her.*
She's not usually like this. Underneath it all,
my better self wants to marry me, but she thinks
I'm not worthy. She nicknames me Sweetie,
I nickname her B.S. for Better Self.
When I want to bite like a black fly,
she gets there first and blows kisses.
Can't anyone see how awful she is?
She says, *You can come out now. Whoops,*
only joking. I snarl with a mouth full of maggots.
She says, *listen to me or you're on your own*
and everyone will know what you're really like.
She says, *Don't talk back.*

Before we leave for the protest,
my better self cuts her eyes at me:
When you go to the rally, chant,
pump your sign if you must,
but don't pick anyone's pocket.
When she turns her back, I slip
her wallet out of her bag.

My better self insists we go to counseling.
She wants to work things out.
When the therapist asks, *And how do you feel
about that?* I shrug, while my better self sniffles
and rubs her cheek. *We're getting a divorce,* I say,
*and I'm taking the car and leaving
our issues unresolved because I don't want
to prolong this any longer than yesterday.*
Meaning, I took the keys from the counter,
the engine is running, have a nice life.

HIS ANSWER

I lean forward trying to keep up
conversation as I watch my father
make himself eat. At ninety-six
he struggles to maintain his weight.
Forty minutes for a tiny sandwich,
a speck of salad. Then cake, ice cream,
whipped cream, chocolate sauce.
I can't taste anything, he tells me. *Only desserts.*
The sweet taste buds are the last to go.

He's still shipshape, my father,
the marine engineer. Every morning
he showers, shaves, dresses himself.
I used to be handy, he says.
I went around and fixed things
for everyone. Now it takes two people
to help me in and out of the car.
I don't want to be bedridden.

And what can I say,
the mouthy child, who started this
by asking what he looks forward to
each day? *Nothing,* he shrugs,
I've outlived myself.

MY FATHER FLOATING

My father floats
in a fearful dream, rises
outside his body,
but he's stuck
in the living room, which appears
tilted at a surreal angle, ceiling fan
coming out of a wall. *Float*
somewhere nicer, my sister suggests.
Havana, Athens, Cairo, places he traveled
as a younger man, extra pages stapled
into his passport in accordion folds.
Or maybe visit that East Hampton bungalow
we used to rent before it became
such a fashionable address.

Help, help, he cries
arms flailing. Perched on a ledge
about to go over, he can't find the floor,
though he's upright, secure, and awake
in his chair. The usual laws
no longer apply. The structures
that house him, the very habits themselves,
relinquish their long service.
Coaxing, demanding, our voices
fade to distant traffic, our faces
vague moons. *I've been out of my body,*
he tells us at lunch, as we attend
to his labored breathing, keep trying
to fix his feet to the ground.

DRY DOCK

Drydocked beyond repair
in his fancy Barcalounger,
my father couldn't fix himself
the way he fixed tankers,
made their engines roar and glow.

For two nights I kept watch
as he slept, reassured if he groaned,
alarmed if his breath quieted,
just as he, on a cruise, slept
through our giggles, slept
through suitcases sliding
across the cabin floor in rough seas
but woke with a start when the engine
grew muffled as we scraped
through the Straits of Corinth.

                    * * *

Now he occupies the space a ship
leaves in its wake or the gaps
between gang plank steps so wide
that I, as a child, was afraid I'd slip through.

                    * * *

I'm a stuttering engine,
a ship whose rudder is tangled in rope.

I can't stay in drydock forever,
a tanker not sure what port
it's bound for. The captain
asleep. The engineer
aimlessly checking the valves.

AFTER A PAINTING BY QUINTON OLIVER JONES

Largo dolcemente con assarazza ma con amaleleta

I am a stunned bird lost among pencil thin trees.
A musical staff, like a permeable fence, stretched
above, below; notes scattered in the landscape
like jack-in-the pulpits, notes I might sing
if I were a bird with a song. The birches lean
as though a small wind brushed by, but there is no wind,
only quiet and one short flight
stopped. I was once that girl asleep
on the strong branch of the oak, a girl almost as long
as the trunk of the tree where she rests, as the limb
where she dreams the same dream over and over
mistaking it for a life. Has she confused this passivity
with serenity or sleep with enchantment?

The moments we compose, the least truthful of all.
Like the moment I composed for my father's death
with his help: In August he told me he wanted to die,
which he did, and at home, where he did. In December,
he urged me to wait until April to visit. We all knew
there'd be no April but didn't want him to know
we knew. We were birds stopped
midflight, silenced.

At the end he was frightened. His constricted voice
forcing out *death, dying.* Then he became the mute swan
in this framed pastel painting or perhaps the mauve bird
in the stunted black tree with no leaves, watching the girl
asleep in the thick oak and the musical notes stuck
here and there like stories we don't want to tell.
In this sleeping girl's first dream, a child she adores

is sucked down a drainpipe into the basement
like a letter down a pneumatic tube.
When she rushes below, she can't see or hear him.
The plumber can't find him. Is he trapped in the wall?
Is he deep in the earth? (Might he be her father?)
In the next dream, her father returns. He didn't want to die after all,
and being a man of ingenuity and discipline, willed himself
back into the living room, twenty years younger.
And the child? He's right down the street riding his bike
with his friends, poking at a dead squirrel then squealing
and running home. Perhaps that's the song she will choose.
Let the rest of the notes fall away.

OVER AND OVER

Eternalism argues past, present, future are equally real. Combine that with reincarnation, and I could be living multiple lives without knowing it. I just happen to be conscious of the dullest one, which I make even duller by never leaving the house voluntarily or without regret. But if I could leave for one of those other lives? Maybe the one in a seaside town in Northern Maine where I clam, catch lobsters and know everyone at the bar. Or Barcelona where I meet my secret lover each afternoon in a cafe on Las Ramblas and leave my espresso untouched. Maybe Chicago, a chambermaid supporting four kids on her tips. I didn't say these lives were easier, did I? Just more intense. But I'm only aware of being in this suburban movie, preparing a birthday party for my grown daughter who has given me attitude for spoiling the surprise her husband planned but forgot to tell me about. I silently apologize to my own mother for all the backtalk I gave her over nothing. It's too late to ask forgiveness unless she too is living another life in which she still remembers who I am. As for my daughter, I had such a long labor, two days, so much hard pushing, but no matter which life I might be in, once the contractions begin things move in a single direction, so already I've lost control.

Maybe the surprise will be that when they arrive, I'll be gone leaving the big white cake with whipped cream and strawberries next to a note on the table saying "moved to a parallel universe. No forwarding address." All lives begin with some woman pushing some other life out of her and end with that life rising out of its body or with a *phht* like a deflating balloon, like my mother's which she forgot while she was living it. After she died, she was ashes, and I'm grateful I didn't have to choose one outfit from all her clothes then see her laid out like a doll in a box, didn't risk confusing the scent of mortuary flowers with her Chanel Number 5. I'm glad I can imagine she's simply moved to another life having carelessly misplaced this one.

Believe me, I know there is only this life of bickering family and my own touchy self. *I was nervous,* my daughter apologizes. She doesn't like to be the center of attention. After twenty-nine years, how did I forget that? Despite good intentions, we elbow each other's bruises again and again. Eternalism's a kind of trap, no escape. Over and over the dead stay dead. Might as well tear up that fantasy note. Bring out the cake. Light the candles. Could extinguishing their small, cheerful flames possibly make wishes come true? We sing happy birthday once more.

ALL OF US

George Washington chases his false teeth
through space. All of us, living and dead,
weightless as astronauts, floating: Elizabeth I,
with her receding hairline, Genghis Khan
linking arms with the North Cambridge cobbler.
My friend, Phyllis, spins by so fast she can't hear
me call out. Even baby Emory, so very alive,
floating arms outstretched, shouts for his brother
to look. My elementary school nuns have lost
their wimples and veils though their black habits
flap like the wings of distressed crows.
I'm getting dizzy and wondering how long this will last
and whether I like it or not. Exciting at first,
but I can't steer at all. I'm just a slip of paper
caught by wind or a cotton shirt churning
in the washing machine. Let the dead float happy
and gravity pull the rest of us back to the ground.

NIGHT SKY

Our troubles show up like stars disturbing
the blank night, petty compared to the moon—
jewel in a black velvet case—but grouped
in constellations, what satisfying tales.
The big and little dippers quench our thirst
to be tragic as Callisto, turned by Juno to a bear.
Likewise we've been wronged by a jealous lover's fear
or, like Andromeda, ruined by a parent's pride
then rescued just in time, or so we like to say
to make our lives exciting, at least significant
as stars we map our passage by, a story
we can squint at, something with a shape.

BEQUEST

I give my legs to the ray that prowls the bottom
Let them be its stilts; my eyes to the oysters
My hair becomes rockweed, my ribs
Grow slippery with moss
Fingers thin to stinging anemone
Knees, to rocks near the shore
And my teeth to barnacles clinging
My lungs are hermaphrodite sponges
Gobies hide in the cave of my mouth
I place my eggs in the sea skate's purse
My ears burrow and close like clams
Buttocks become two horseshoe crabs
My clitoris a shy mussel, my vulva a sea snail
Now my breasts float, two jellyfish
My feet lengthen to tentacles of squid
My tongue slithers, a muscular eel
The manatee's thick flippers—my arms and my belly
My shoulder blades cut through the water
The tides of my blood released
Breath laps the shore
And the salt of my body dissolves

RAIN

My grandson laughs at rain's thrum
on his windbreaker's hood, while I grumble,
pinch my thumb in the foldable
umbrella's broken spring. Try to force it,
fail, distracted by the rambunctious child's
puddle stomping, the mumbling
hum of his rain song. Why not
raise my face to sky's wet tumble?

Notes

"Croagh Patrick"—Reek Sunday is the last Sunday in July.

"Liberty Hotel Boston"—The full attribution for the epigraph and the term "jailness" is Ann Coppola, *Lockdown Luxury*, published 9/24/2007 on corrections. com. The phrase "where vestiges of original cells create cozy nooks" can be round on luxurytraveladvisor.com on the Liberty Hotel Boston website.

The reference to Buddhist monks blessing the hotel is from "Best of Boston All Stars: What's New at the Liberty Hotel" by Vanessa Nason, *Boston Magazine*, 1/13/2016.

"At Sixteen Months: Brown and Gold" is for Emory Smith.

"Negative Space" is for Abby Freedman.

"Self-Portrait as Sun Washed"—Sun Washed is the name of a Benjamin Moore paint color and the epigraph is taken from the Benjamin Moore online paint catalog.

"Self-Portrait as the Two of Swords" is for Kathy DeZengotita.

"Rain" is for Damion Smith.

Acknowledgments

Grateful acknowledgment is made to the editors of the following journals in which these poems or versions of them first appeared.

Apprentice to Light: the West of Ireland. Glen McClure. Norfolk, VA: Parke Press, 2020: "Croagh Patrick"

Anchor: "Self-Portrait as River"

The Cincinnati Review: "He"

Ibbetson Street Magazine: "Bequest," "Praise for the Ill," "Fear Street," "Difficult Child"

LEON Literary Review: "All Saints Eve, 2019," "My Better Self"

Lily Poetry Journal: "After a Painting by Quinton Oliver Jones"

MER VOX: "The Empty Boat Speaks," "Self-Portrait as Geranium," "Self-Portrait as Sunrise"

Molecule: a tiny lit mag: version of "Self-Portrait as Geranium"

The Ocean State Review: "Liberty Hotel"

Pangyrus online: "His Answer"

Pendemic: "Negative Space"

Pinyon: "Self-Portrait as Angry Dog"

The Progressive: "You"

Quick Fiction: "Spying"

Salamander: "Night Sky"

Solstice Lit Mag: "My Father Floating," "World Happiness Index, 2019"

Stone Canoe: "Self-Portrait as the Two of Swords"

West Texas Literary Review: "At Sixteen Months: Brown and Gold"

Women Artists Datebook 2022. Syracuse Cultural Workers. "Self-Portrait as a Seagull"

Many thanks to Steve Huff and Phil Memmer for their support of this book. To Glen McClure for the cover photograph and to Marshall McClure for her input in cover design. To my workshop group: Suzanne Berger, Christopher Corkery, Erica Funkhouser, Helena Minton who read and reread every poem in this book. To Mary Amsler, Robin Becker, LR Berger, Ceila Glibert, Barbara Helfgott Hyett, Leslie Lawrence, Andee Rubin for their friendship and encouragement. To MP Carver, Kevin Carey, Lis Horowitz, Kali Lightfoot, Jennifer Jean, Jennifer Martelli, Colleen Michaels, January O'Neil, Dawn Paul, JD Scrimgeour, and Cindy Veach for welcoming me into the North Shore writers' community. To Meg Kearney, Anne-Marie Oomen, Dzvinia Orlowsky, Sandra Scofield and to all the faculty and students of the Solstice MFA in Creative Writing Program. To the egregore, you know who you are. And to Richard, always.

About the Author

Kathleen Aguero has published several collections of poetry: *After That, Daughter Of, The Real Weather, Thirsty Day, Investigations: The Mystery of the Girl Sleuth,* a collection of poems inspired by Nancy Drew. Her work has appeared in numerous literary journals, including *Poetry* magazine, *The Massachusetts Review,* and *The Cincinnati Review.* She is also co-editor of three collections of multicultural literature: *A Gift of Tongues, An Ear to the Ground,* and *Daily Fare.* Her creative nonfiction essay "Marriage Koan" appears in the anthology *Why I'm Still Married.* Recipient of a Massachusetts Fellowship in Poetry and a fellowship to the Virginia Center for the Creative Arts, Kathleen also was awarded a writing grant from the Elgin/Cox Trust. She has taught at the Writers' Center at the Chautauqua Institute in upstate New York, the NY State Young Writers' Program at Skidmore, as well as in the Poets in the Schools Programs of New Hampshire and Massachusetts. In 2004, she held the position of Visiting Research Associate at the Brandeis University Women's Studies Research Center in Waltham, Massachusetts. In addition to teaching in the Solstice MFA program, Kathleen teaches for "Changing Lives Through Literature," an alternative sentencing program based on the power of books to change lives through reading and group discussion. She is a consulting editor in poetry for *The Kenyon Review.*

Colophon

The text of *World Happiness Index* is set in Minion.
This trade edition was printed by BookMobile in Minneapolis, MN.

Publication of this book was made possible through
the generous contributions of the following donors:

Michael Ansara

Jeanne Marie Beaumont

The Bishop Butler Society

Laure-Anne Bosselaar Brown

Charles Cote

Debra Kang Dean

Celia and Walter Gilbert

Kathleen Knisely

Tony Leuzzi

Mike Lew & Thom Harrigan

Deena Linett

Tim Madigan

Wendy Mnookin

Teresa Sutton

David Weiss

More Poetry from Tiger Bark Press